you rock mae!

Kaitlin ♡

Wag Moe!

♡ Kellen Ann

DAISY

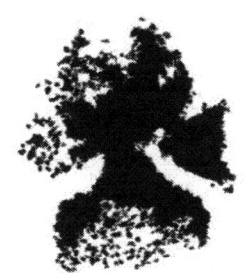

ROCCO

MAX

GUS

LORETTA

Publisher: Cards That Wow!, Inc.
Imprint: Cards That Wow!

Copyright 2023
Kellen A. Fisher©
All Rights Reserved

Pugs That Wow! Inc.
www.pugsthatwow.com

Library of Congress Control Number
2023902460

Printed in the USA

Illustrated and Designed by Jenn Garside

ISBN
979-8-9876908-0-2

First Edition

WAG MORE!

Life lessons learned from observing my grumble

written by
KELLEN ANN

DEDICATION

When I sat down to dedicate this book a swirl of panic welled in my head. What if I forget someone was the biggest fear that floated up to the top of my psyche. Then I realized that I couldn't possibly include everyone that had an impact on me completing this book. Chances are if you are reading it I am indebted to you and grateful. This book is the culmination of decades of life's experiences and relationships that have seamlessly come to a head in the pages you are about to read. So with that being said, I thank you right at this moment.

There are a few people that have stood out during this process and the first and foremost would be my daughter Emily. She probably had more faith that I could finish this project than anyone else in my life. I know this because she has lived through the chaos, tears, laughter, and, most importantly, the victories. With that being said, Emily, I thank you for standing by me, and not making me feel stupid for writing a self-help book using the Grumble as my vehicle. Thank you for making this happen and for humorously referring to me as your senile wackadoodle mother, in the utmost respectful way, when describing me to your friends.

You know when an olympian is standing on the pedestal and they are about to receive their medal? Then you see them mouth the words "Thanks Mom!"? Well, to me, this is that moment. I am now standing on the podium and thanking you, Mom, for your love and support during this entire process.

I would be remiss if I left out my #Megamind Family, Jeffrey and Jennifer Gitomer, and Steve Rizzo. Add in all my Write that Book Masterclass friends and we complete the circle. All of whom continued to cheer me on and get me to the finish line.

Lastly, I would like to acknowledge Michael Heppell. Your Write That Book Pop-Up and then your Masterclass were the catalyst that gave me the tools to make this happen in a professional way while still allowing me to maintain integrity in telling my story.

FORWARD

Ever notice how dogs shake it off? You know, after they have an encounter out of the norm, something that may induce stress, they shake it off literally from nose to tail.

This was one of the best lessons my dogs taught me. As humans, we tend to freeze (hello, fight or flight) in stressful situations. Most people stop their breath from going low and slow and that impairs your ability to respond well. But, what if you could move that stuck energy and shake it off like a dog? Your ability to react, respond and recover in those anxious moments would be way better.

Taylor Swift's *Shake it off* may have a whole new meaning now. Cue the dance moves! The next time you see your dog shaking it off, may it be your reminder to shake your hands, shake your body and let go of what is weighing you down so that you can reset like a dog.

When Kellen Ann told me she was writing this book, *Wag More!* I knew she was the perfect person to write about pugs and their life lessons.

Kellen Ann is not just an amazing mom, but also the ultimate dog mom. You may know Kellen Ann from her former blog, *Pug Lady Rules of Life*, which resulted in over 70,000 followers. Followers who waited for her next thoughts and writings like a dog wanting a bone.

There's a reason why: Kellen Ann is the go-to pug gal. And there is no one better positioned than Kellen Ann to write this book. She provides insightful, real-world help that will enable you to see the world with a new lens.

This tail-wagging self-help book will remind you of the little ways dogs impart wisdom. It will increase your gratitude, improve your resilience and remind you of your unconditional love.

Dogs teach you something new every day and the best lessons are contained in this book. If you want to learn more about life's lessons, leashes and unconditional love get a dog and read this book.

If you're a dog lover, you will easily relate to the messages Kellen Ann provides and the insightful lessons her grumbles teach. If you know a dog lover, this book is the perfect gift.

Speaking of gifts...When I got my first dog, I knew I would be taking care of her, but I didn't realize she would be taking care of me. Getting me to "paws," be more with nature, go on daily walks, learn how to shake off the bad stuff, and most importantly, to love and be loved unconditionally. Your dog has likely given you the same gift.

8,760. One of the biggest gifts Charlie has given me. 8,760 walks. I've taken Charlie out roughly 8,760 times. That's 8,760 times to be grateful, to stop and smell the roses, and take a break from digital screens and virtual meetings. And a whole lot of steps.

Even in the rain, snow, and freezing cold. But hey, that's unconditional love.

Question: Do you ever think to yourself, "I have to take my dog on a walk"?

Realize this: You don't have to. You get to.

Now read on and Wag More!

Woof, **Jen Gitomer**
Best-selling author and Dog Mom

INTRODUCTION

This is the story of how Rocco, Daisy, Gus, Loretta, and Max, my smushy-faced Grumble, helped me see life in a whole new way. How they were instrumental in the healing of my mind, my body, and most importantly, my soul.

As I write this introduction, laying on the couch to the left of me is Gus, who is snorkeling louder than I have ever heard before. Rocco is laying on the floor dreaming. I know this because he is yipping and running in place. It is very fun to watch. And Max is right here on my lap and whenever I need to hit the delete button on my keyboard, I have to reposition his curly tail.

This is my life AP. (After Pugs). And to be honest, I couldn't imagine it any other way. Yes, my days are filled with three distinct personalities, a festival of bodily functions and noises, but most of all, the most amazing unconditional love I have ever felt.

This is why, when I was at the lowest point in my life, abused, fearful, self-hating, with low to no confidence, I unknowingly turned to my Pugs.

I started observing them. Watching how they reacted to things. How they pushed on even when times were difficult. But most of all, I learned to stop and reflect before I reacted, not allow myself to engage with negativity, and most importantly, I learned to laugh at myself. I do this a lot by the way.

Enjoy each chapter, as they have lessons learned or observations made that have contributed to my life in not only different ways but in the most joyous of ways. I hope you find this book fun and entertaining but most of all I hope it will help you stop and smell the pork chops, be kind to yourself, and most importantly, Wag More!

CONTENTS

(OF A PUG)

CHAPTER 1
MEET THE GRUMBLE

First, you need to meet the Grumble. The Pugs that I have observed in order to write this book of healing. While some have crossed the rainbow bridge, they are still very important to some of my lessons. It is important that know that all my Pugs are rescues. The misfits of the Pug world that have lovingly become my grumble. In case you don't know, a grumble is when you have 3 or more Pugs. Look it up, this is a real thing.

First, meet Rocco. Rocco is the Pug that started it all. He was my first Pug, and he is lovingly referred to as the PBP. (Poorly Bred Pug). He is a tiny guy with the biggest heart. He is somewhat neurotic, and I am his service person. I even have my very own orange vest I wear when we go on walks. He definitely beats to a different drummer, but heck, that is what makes him so unique. I'll never forget the first time my aunt saw him. The first words out of her mouth were, "he's a humper!" and she was spot on.

Next, we have Daisy. Rest in peace my sweet Daisy. She was the matriarch of the Pug tribe and came complete with the most distinguishing underbite. Daisy truly adored me, and I could feel her love every time she looked up at me. I'm not going to lie; the day she crossed the rainbow bridge I lost a big part of my heart. It still hurts to this day. She is the namesake of my nonprofit and the Pug that taught me the most.

Now Gus & Loretta arrived together. They were rescued from a puppy mill in Oakland, California. A shelter near my home knew that I rescued Pugs, so they contacted me as soon as their smushy faces arrived at the shelter. There was an outbreak of parvo and they needed to get the Pugs out as soon as possible. So, to my humble abode, they were delivered.

Gus is a true Gus. He is a big lug and another Pug with a huge heart. Gus was so frightened when he came to our house. It is a known fact that he didn't have any toys where he came from, as a matter of fact, he had never been outside or even knew how to walk on a leash. But back to the toys... It wasn't long before he discovered these small yellow balls; you know the Kong ones. I would throw one for him, and he would run around the couch for 20 min. I'm serious, we timed him. He caught on the fetch part but not the bring the ball back part. He made the craziest sound of glee as he was running around that couch.

Now, meet Loretta (pronounced Lor-Re-Tahhh!). RIP sweet Lo-Re-Tahhhh. She was certainly made from a different mold. She was a textbook female Pug with her beautiful fawn (actually peach) color fur, round eyes, and smushy face. She was so poorly malnourished that she only came to me with 2 teeth. But that did not slow her carnivorous appetite. It was a common joke around the house that if there were an Apocalypse, we would follow her for she was a skilled forger. Another fun fact, we all believed that she would chew through your arm to get to a pork chop.

Max, (pronounced Max) is the newest addition to the Grumble. My daughter felt that after Loretta crossed the rainbow bridge, It was a necessity to find another Pug to keep my license plate accurate. (3PUGMOM) He too is a rescue. He came complete with a cleft palate and a disproportioned front leg. This does not slow him down at all. He is a regular dynamo. The funniest, most misunderstood Pug you could ever know. Again, a heart the size of Texas and the energy of my daughter on 5 Redbulls.

Now that you know what the definition of a grumble is and you have officially met mine, I am very excited to share with you the wisdom and life lessons learned from observing The Grumble.

You remember what that is, right?

Tail End: There are so many definitions of "family". To some it is blood, to some it is longevity, some it is even a chance meeting that turns into something substantial. If I have learned anything it is that it is certainly a combination of all of these. The people, and pets that have created my family unit are all from very unexpected experiences. Don't let a definition keep you from curating your perfect family or Grumble.

CHAPTER 2
THE SCIENTIFIC STUFF

This wouldn't be a real book about life transformation if it didn't include some sort of personality test, right? Well, here is my attempt to make this chapter of the book the official personality study part of the book. This will make some of the actions of the Grumble make more sense. It will also try to prove the long-time myth that dogs eventually start to resemble their humans and possibly, vice versa.

If that statement is true, then It won't happen soon enough for me! Rocco is as stealthy as an Olympic track and field sprinter, so when that transformation finally occurs to my current figure you will see one very happy Pug Mom right here! Anyway, this got me thinking. "Is it possible for the dogs to develop similar personalities as their human companions"? Do we change to the Pug personality or does the Pug change to ours?

I thought to myself, wouldn't it be interesting to see if our personalities matched those of the Pugs who bonded with us? This reminded me of a good friend, Carol, who gave me a personality test at a retreat she hosted a million years ago. It was great, it taught me my personality strengths and how to use them in my sales career. It also taught me how to define another person's personality and in the process made me a top salesperson. Anyway, this amazing and dynamic woman was a tiny package that delivered one heck of a bang! She introduced me to the art and benefits of the personality test.

So, this then led me to the internet for research. I decided to find a personality test that I could take and then take it and answer the questions how I thought Rocco would answer them. I then gave the test to Loretta's Pug dad. Finally, I gave the test to my daughter, and she answered for Gus.

I chose the Meyers and Briggs style test because is the most common and respected personality test and it was only 12 minutes to take. Yeah, 12 minutes...Riiiggghhttt!

Do you have any idea how hard it is to get three people and three Pugs to sit still long enough to take a Meyers and Briggs style Personality test???????

These test studies included the four functions, listed below. According to the test, each person prefers one of these cognitive functions and finds it most natural to rely on it in everyday situations. You take the test then you get a four-letter rating.

Introversion (I) or Extroversion (E): where you get your energy from. Intuition (N) or Sensing (S): how you prefer to take in information. Thinking (T) or Feeling (F): how you make decisions. Judging (J) or Perceiving (P): the way you choose to order your life.

We are all a combination of all of the above; however, we have a natural tendency to find it more natural to rely on one of the two in everyday situations. There are 16 combinations of the letters when you take the test to get a four-letter result: your MBTI type.

I am an ENFJ and Rocco is an ENFP. Rocco and I are both extroverts, intuitive and assertive. There was only a 6% difference in our score. That really did not surprise me. I found this to be quite accurate, except for the body type. We both get distracted very easily, we both like to sleep in, we both sniff our food before we eat it and we both ABSOLUTELY HATE CHANGE. ENFP's are fiercely independent and crave creativity and freedom.

Rocco is definitely creative, especially when he eats. This is usually a 37 min process. He will circle the dish 2 or 10 times, sniff with each lap, circle some more, back up, circle one more time, and then finally take very tiny bites. Can't get much more creative than that, right? We are both leaders, so it is no wonder that many famous ENFJ's & P's are Presidents. This personality type wants to lead the way to a brighter future! Yup, that is us indeed! Oh, wouldn't it be great to see Rocco's name on a presidential ballot??

My Daughter is an ENFJ and Gus is an ISFJ. What is interesting about this is that while they don't match as well as Rocco and me, they were exactly the same on the FJ, Feeling and Judging, part of the test. They are both feelers and judgers. They engage their emotions, they act on ideas, and they follow rules and regulations.

Following rules and regulations really stand out most in my mind about them. Gus is very OCD when it comes to playing. He has a certain toy and a certain path. If you block the path. it completely throws him into a Pug frenzy. Then he starts making his funny humming noises and we have to make his path clear before his head explodes.

Emily is the same way when it comes to certain things too. Especially her horse. Things must be done in a certain order, or her head will explode too. These two may not be on the presidential ballot but they both have the potential to change the world. Plus, they both probably could convince you to vote for Rocco!

Last but not least for this experiment was Loretta and her Pug Dad. He is an ESTP and Loretta is an ENTP. Again, the first two traits were no matches, but the last two were spot on. The TP is for thinking and perceiving. Yes, both Loretta and her dad fit perfectly into this category. They both live in the moment and dive into action. Loretta is a bit more literal in the diving part of this description. She is famous around the house for diving through the air and grabbing food out of Rocco's mouth, mid-chew. She was definitely living that moment and diving...

They are both bold, original, direct, and sociable. They are also both very energetic and charismatic. Direct is another function to describe actions. Yup, Loretta will find the most direct way to food. No deviation from her perceived path she goes directly from point A to point B.

My research didn't show anything really concrete, but it sure was fun learning about our similarities on a semi-scientific level. If you are anything like me, you probably still have some questions. Who changed whom? Although it might be pretentious of me to think that I or any human for that matter could change the personality of a Pug.

The facts remain the same, at five different times five different Pugs gravitated into my life. Do they find me because of a personality attraction? Did they cast a magic spell so that I would find them? All I know is that the five Pugs that I have and had, each gravitated in my direction. So there really may be something about this personality thing.

I am no professional, and this is as far as my personality research will go. So, if you are out and suddenly find yourself gravitating to a puppy adoption area or you see a pup that needs a home on the internet, maybe it is your pup finding you. Don't miss your sign!

Tail End: You never know when or where you are going to meet your Grumble. You know, the one thing in your life that will help you, love you, and be there unconditionally for you! Make sure to pay attention so you don't miss them.

CHAPTER 3
THE ART OF RELAXATION

I, as a Pug owner, have first-hand, living examples of the art of relaxation. So that made me wonder why am I stressed all the time. Face it, we all worry about most of the same stuff like family, our kids, health, finances, self-worth, and on and on.

Some of us probably pay tons of money to join gyms, visit therapists, go to personal coaches, learn yoga, and how to meditate. We even go online, for more hours than we would ever admit subjecting our psyche to programming that puts us in a comatose-nirvana state of mind.

I too, yes me, was guilty of constantly searching for the ultimate way to relax and de-stress. I actually got stressed trying to find a way to decompress.

Then one day, I decided to watch The Grumble. Whenever they seemed to be uptight, stressed, or out of sorts they had their own special way to combat these demons. They had a working model for this, and it was pretty amazing to me.

A stressed Gus will bark at me. Just one bark. This method is usually performed in the middle of the room where the desired person's attention is located. Yes, 90% of the time, it is me. And 100 percent of the time it was in the kitchen. What this could mean is that I did not throw his yellow ball quickly enough, and this is his reminder that we are not done until he says we are done. He will also use the one bark method when he thinks I have forgotten to feed him. He will sit in the middle of the kitchen, bark once, and look obstinate until his food dish is filled and delivered.

A stressed Loretta would pace and stare at you if you didn't feed her soon enough. She liked to express her disappointment and anger with a shrill that would terrify your ears followed by an elongated raspy sigh. I will never be able to describe this in words so just know your ears are forever thankful for not having to hear it. The only things that stressed Loretta were food, lack of food, and delayed delivery of food.

Now Rocco seems to be in a constant state of stress. While I am eating dinner he will sit near the table and literally vibrates because he wants a bite of my dinner so badly. He also makes a noise that I can't even describe. He also stresses about sitting in the chair with me, going on walks, car rides, loud noises, being alone, being with too many people, other dogs, and balloons. That being said he too has a strategy to keep himself from exploding or having a doggie stroke.

You can go online and find hundreds of links that will give you scientific techniques and some pretty quirky ways to relax. I feel it best to give you the suggestions that I learned from The Grumble and try to follow in my daily life.

Here are the 5 ways I have observed and implemented into my daily routine to relax like a Pug.

1. Take a deep Pugbreath: Have you ever noticed how a Pug, just before they fall asleep, takes a deep breath in and snort out its nose? Try it, it works. I see it as getting all the bad air out and it shooting directly out your nose. Take note, the bad air translates into snot as it comes out, so it is best to have a tissue handy.

2. Pugitation: It is similar to meditation, but it is Pug-style. Loretta does this more than the other Pugs. She sits up straight, her nose pointed toward the ceiling, it appears that she clears her mind and then does a circular motion just before she falls over and takes a nap. I have done the same thing. Even though I rock more than move in the circular motion, I still fall over and end up taking a 20-minute nap. I don't recommend that you do this at work though.

3. Pugxercise: Every now and then Rocco and Max will run laps around the dining room table. They go and go and go. Suddenly they stop, shake their head, and then chug over to their favorite nap areas and, you guessed it, they take a snooze. Yes, on occasion I run laps around my dining room table too. I pretend each lap is a quarter mile and I feel really accomplished.

4. Pugratitude: There isn't a day that goes by that my little Pugs don't look at me with a sincere look of Pugratitude. I know that by rescuing them I saved them from terrible conditions. In their loving way, they show me this every day and now I do the same. I am thankful for all the wonderful things going on in my life and it just makes me feel better to dwell on the good things instead of the negative.

5. Pugtherapy: You know when they follow you all over the house and outside and travel constantly in your blind spot? Well, that is them telling you that they need you and you need them. Take 5 or 20 or 60 minutes to just sit with them. The best relaxation technique in my regime is sitting with my Pugs and listening to them snorkel, snore, and even purrrrr. (Rocco is the purrer). I can't describe the feeling of calm and the feeling that all is good in the world.

Tail End: As you can see, there are no expensive doctors to see, you don't have to change your diet or see a relaxation professional. The key is to make time for yourself and enjoy your pets. Believe me, they love sitting on your lap snoogling and snorting with you more than anything in the world. And doesn't it feel good to know that you are helping them relax, too?

CHAPTER 4
THE ART OF APPRECIATION

Gratitude, thankfulness, gratefulness, or appreciation is a feeling or attitude in acknowledgment of a benefit that one has received or will receive. Thank you, Wikipedia. In common terms, it is something that makes you feel like nothing else. It is a bundle of happiness in your heart that explodes and just makes you want to be a better person.

Do you think Pugs know this definition? If you take a look at my Grumble, you will see the most grateful and thankful dogs in the world. Every day they show me thanks and love in a magnitude of ways. I don't think it is a learned response. It just seems to be natural to them.

I'm pretty sure they are happy with the lifestyle they have been provided, and it is apparent that they have adapted very well over the past few years. There is nothing more awesome than to see that gleam in their eyes that is unexplainable. This leads me to believe that it is more than the obvious things that they are truly thankful for.

If you were to ask Loretta, she would be thankful for the hot water we pour over her food to make it soft and easier for her two-toothed mouth to eat. She would be thankful for us allowing her to gnaw on us, up and down our arms like an ear of corn to massage her gums every morning and every evening. She would also be thankful for the fuzzy blanket at the end of the bed for her to snuggle in each night.

If you were to ask Gus, I'm pretty sure he would put someone to play fetch with at the top of his list. He spends all day and evening dropping toys at our feet to be thrown and loyally brings them back to be thrown again and again and again. Don't get me wrong, he is also pretty thankful for the yummy dog kibble, the California King bed and I certainly should not leave out his every morning ritual of herding Rosie and Riley, my 2 horses.

Rocco, sweet Rocco. You know how people have companion dogs? Well, Rocco is probably most grateful for me, his Companion Person. I finally got my own orange vest that I wear when we are out together. He is so nervous, and he is happy to have me fight his battles. For example, every meal I defend his right to eat and protect his food from the other two Pugs. Not only do I serve as protector, I also follow him around the house for a minimum of 15 minutes while he decides on the safest and most comfortable place to eat. While this may seem extreme to you, it is just our way of life, and I am happy to make him feel secure.

Max shows his gratitude like no other. It is usually in a sprint. From out of nowhere he will run towards me at what seems like 100mph. I've learned to protect my face because you never know where he is going to land. But, when he does, I can see in his face the total happiness and gratitude he feels for me. He has no concept of personal boundaries, but I don't care. He is just another grateful Pug.

As this chapter comes to a close, the sounds of three Pugs emmiting amazingly loud snores and snorkels in the background. This confirms that these are the obvious things that they would be most thankful for if they could speak. While they may not be grateful for all the photos I take, and the sometimes silly hats they are given to wear, be sure they realize it is a small price to pay for their charmed and enchanted life.

The one thing that they all agree on is that they are grateful to be rescued. To have a loving family who accepts all their idiosyncrasies, noises, and smells and is happy to love us, humans, as much, or more, as we love them.

Tail End: I am just as thankful to them for the joy, laughter, and loud Pug noises that they have added to my life. What do you think your doggies are thankful for?

CHAPTER 5
THE ART OF CONFIDENCE

I had been a volunteer art teacher for grades K-5 for over 15 years. Talk about life lessons...

It surprised me to discover that up until the 3rd grade the kids never said, "Oh, I can't draw", "I can't even draw a stick figure", and "I can't draw a straight line". What is it that happens between the end of the 3rd grade and the beginning of 4th that makes the kiddos lose their confidence?

As some get older it starts to become stressful for a child to participate in art! I know, that sounds crazy, but it is true. I just wonder if it is from the environment where they grow up? Is it their personality type? Genetics? Where does peer pressure come from? I'm no doctor or professional by any means, but it always made me wonder.

Here is how The Grumble deals with peer pressure, the environment, and basic confidence breakers. It is quite simple as you will soon find out.

Max, for example, is in what would be called his toddler stage. His goals are simple but mighty and he has no fear of accomplishing them.

First, do not let ANYONE sit in my lap without him. Second, do not let me pet or show affection to any other Pug in the home without him. Third, do not let anyone play with ANY toy because they are now all his property.

Like the pre-4th grader, he is fearless in his pursuit to attain each of these goals. He divebombs the other Pugs, he has been known to drag Rocco by his hind leg to remove him from his space in the living room. I've seen Max fly through the air, literally, he flew over my head, to take a toy away from Gus. His confidence has not waned in any way, but am curious to see what happens when he leaves this stage of his puppyhood. I really doubt things will change at all.

Now if these kiddos could take a lesson from Loretta, my female Pug i.e., Queen of the World. They wouldn't be pressured by setting standards that are unattainable and worry about the pursuit to be perfect.

Loretta is a KLUTZ! She doesn't pay attention to where she is walking and is constantly running into things. Does she get embarrassed? Of Course not! Does she care what anyone thinks? Nope. Does she lose sight of her goal? Not at all!

One time her Pug dad was sitting in his chair working on his laptop and she took a running leap onto his lap and crashed right into the back of his computer. She landed safely on the ground, shook her head, and looked at him as if to say, "Hey, move the computer! Can't you see that I'm trying to jump on your lap"!

If Loretta had felt that she had made a fool out our herself by trying to jump on her dad's lap and gave up because she felt inadequate, she would never have been able to take that 2-hour nap on her dad's lap. BTW, he got a stiff shoulder because of the way he had to hold his computer to accommodate her desire to snooze.

Tail End: My point is to Take notice of your Grumble. Set your goal, don't be afraid to fail, do what it takes to achieve, and most importantly have fun in the process. Don't worry about what other people think and if you fail, keep on trying. If your goal is worth it, you will find a way to make it happen. How else do you think Max has a pile of toys that he stacks under my desk at my feet?

CHAPTER 6
THE ART OF COMMUNICATION

Communication encompasses 99% of all of the problems of our world, in our relationships, our careers, child-raising, and I could go on. How do you master it? Easily...take a look at my Grumble.

I realize that sitting is not something that you really spend much time thinking about, right? We don't study sitting. We just do it. I'm going on a bit of a limb here and I know it is a bit of a stretch comparing sitting to communication but humor me a while and I will make this analogy work.

As far as sitting, I have two sitting positions. I try to sit up straight at the dinner table, meetings, coffee shops, etc. basically whenever I am in public. I'm sure passers-by say, "What wonderful posture she has!" Now when I am in the privacy and confines of my home in my comfy chair or couch, I scrunch down with my chin in my chest and feet propped up. This also makes for a comfy place for the Pugs to sit too.

Now for the Pug part of this chapter. For many, the first thing that you do when you get a puppy is to try to teach them to sit. And don't we feel so proud and accomplished when we do? And the pup is usually so glad to please.

This is true unless you have a Pug. I have read in many articles that Pugs are extremely difficult to train. Not impossible, but you would need the patience of Job and the alignment of Pluto to the moon is the third full phase of the equinox to accomplish the tiniest of successes. This is where communication comes into the mix.

Rocco came to us as a pup and I was able to teach him to sit relatively easily. Well, not really sit like his fanny actually touching the ground below him, he did more of a hover. I was so happy that it was as close to a sit that I thought he would ever complete. I was thrilled with this and figured it best to quit while I was ahead. I was delighted with achieving that!

Gus and Loretta were different stories. As you know, they came from a puppy mill and had no training or manners to speak of. When I could get his attention, Gus would just stare at me like I was some crazy woman. "What are you thinking trying to teach me something? Just stop it and throw the ball woman!" I am sure that is what he was communicating to me!

Loretta didn't even have the decency to sit and stare at me. She just gave me the "Pug Eye" as she trotted away in her indignant way. I mean I could never express the disrespect in her saunter as she walked away with a loud snort in the complete opposite of my request! I do think she gained great pleasure in my defeat.

Max, well Max is, Max. If I can get his attention, which is rare. I get ready to give him the command and before I can even finish, he has sprinted toward something shiny. He may remember to come back to me but have no idea of what I wanted in the first place. Then it turns into a game of smoke and mirrors where I then forget what I originally wanted him to do, and I end up throwing his toys until my arm falls off.

Then one day I realized we had a Pug whisperer in our lives. I went away for the weekend, so my Mom volunteered to watch the Grumble. By the time I got back, she had refined Rocco in his sitting and taught him to ring a bell that was hanging on the door when he needed to go outside. No more hovering for this guy and a poop warning bell all in one! Gus sat like a good boy and Loretta was actually happy to sit. So happy that she wiggled her hiney back and forth with excitement.

When I asked my mom how on earth did she accomplish such a feat, she looked at me very coy and almost condescendingly and said, "I communicated with them". That is it? That is the profound wisdom I had been waiting for from the Pug Whisperer? I was astonished. She reminded me that each Pug had a different personality and all she had to do was be patient with their different learning styles.

Tail End: No matter how your look at it, it is as simple as listening and watching for signals and communication comes naturally. So, the next time your Pup is sitting near you and staring in your direction remember they are communicating with you, and you best stop and take the time to address their current whim in a timely manner.

CHAPTER 7
THE ART OF TELLING THE TRUTH

Possibly Aristotle's most well-known definition of truth is in Metaphysics, (1011b25): "To say of what is that it is not, or of what is not that it is, is false, while to say of what is that it is, and of what is not that it is not, is true".

I'm not sure Pugs even know how to not tell the truth. If you look at it, does any dog try to not tell the truth? I believe this is why we don't stay upset with them very long. They have taken deceit out of the equation and the forgiveness just kicks in automatically.

For example, one of the Pugs took the end of a toilet paper roll and ran out of the bathroom, through the master bedroom, down a long hall, through the dining room and living room, and stopped at the front entry. Now, how did I find out which Pug this was? It was actually quite simple. Rocco was waiting at the door with the end of the TP at his foot and when I looked at him, I asked him, "Did you steal the toilet paper?" he looked up at me and it looked like he was chewing on something. I asked a new question, "are you eating the toilet paper?" and with the most innocent look, he simply nodded. He looked so proud that he had accomplished such a huge task. He didn't know whether to run away or attempt to blame Gus.

My point here is by watching the Pugs deal with potential deceit, they just walk away. They know they are better off biting the bullet, so to speak, and take what wrath may come their way, and then move on to the next part of their Pug day.

I could write an entire three-book series about Max. Again, he doesn't even try to hide the fact that he is a naughty Pug. Or as a friend calls him, a misunderstood Pug. Misunderstood, naughty either way he gets himself into a lot of circumstances. I will admit that nine times out of ten I end up laughing. Ok, ten times out of ten. I have caught Max sitting on the floor chewing something really loud and I look to see that it is not a toy but a pen, my shoe, my makeup, my phone, my mom's phone, boxes, both empty and full, a lampshade, the mail, my pillow, Rocco, and several unidentifiable objects that I can't even imagine where they came from. Does he try to shift the blame? Of course not. He is a Pug.

I have nothing to write about Gus or Loretta. If they have done something that could be construed as naughty, they were smart enough not to get caught. I highly doubt this as they seem to be the Pugs that are too busy napping to get into trouble.

Tail End: Does the Grumble ever try to blame their naughtiness on one of the other Pugs? Nope, they really don't care. They may slightly acknowledge your displeasure but then they will abruptly turn away and move on to the next part of their very hectic schedule.

CHAPTER 8
THE ART OF
EMBRACING CHANGE

Change is something I am not very good at embracing, at all!

Here is a tiny example. One of my besties, Jim, and I would go have coffee every Friday. I drank the same coffee and we sat in the same seats by the window every Friday for as long as I could remember. Then, one day there was a note on the door announcing they would be moving to a new location. What??? Where would we sit? This was truly a dilemma. On the first Friday in the new location, I arrived about 20 min early to scope things out. I found myself in a mental frenzy. When my bestie got there, he calmed me down and chose our new spot. He adapted so easily, me, not so much.

So, if you thought it was hard for me to accept change, imagine what it was like for the Grumble? To say that Pugs are creatures of habit would be a gross understatement.

While adapting to a new home is part of the rescue process, that seemed to be the easy part. It is the ongoing Pug maintenance and overall living that was the tricky part. I'm one that loves to arrange the furniture on a semi-monthly basis. This was something that I had to stop when I became the keeper of a Grumble.

One day I decided to move a small reading chair and an ottoman to a different corner of the living room. Loretta, I guess, was not paying attention, and she took a leap right where the ottoman used to be and landed, smack, on the floor. She was so distraught that she shook her head, snorted a couple of times, and looked at me as if I had just played the cruelest joke on her and that I was conspiring to eliminate her from the family. I'm not sure if she ever got over this but I can tell you that she looked before she leapt from that point on. Mainly because I moved the chair and the ottoman back to the same spot and never moved it again.

Rocco is the epitome of "Don't EVER change anything, EVER"! I made the mistake of moving his food dish. By the look of shock on his little mug, you would have thought I had taken his birthday away! And he REALLY loves birthdays. He was so upset that he refused to eat for 3 days. I tried everything. Hand feeding, pouring some flavorful broth, I even added some chicken.

Nothing worked. If I wasn't careful, I could get in trouble for Pug abuse. If he starved to death, nobody would ever believe that he wouldn't eat because I moved his dish. Right? I did have to give in. I put the dish back and changed my re-arranging plan for that moment. I may try again in 10 or 15 years.

What if I were to change the feeding time here at Chez Grumble? Yeah, don't even think about doing it. Gus is the timekeeper of the meals. He alerts me if I am ever late. He is like a finely tuned grandfather clock that keeps time to the millisecond. I mean 5 pm on the dot his Pug alarm goes off. If I am not in the kitchen, he will certainly let me know that I am forgetting to do the most important task of my life. It is funny because he used to be the same with breakfast. but now, as long as I feed him before noon, he is ok. I think this may be his way of humoring me to think that he has adjusted to a tiny change in the sphere of the universe.

Max really is not aware of any kind of change. I think he missed that line at the puppy lab while he was being assembled. In fact, I think Rocco got Max's helping. Max adapts to EVERYTHING! But we will see as he grows older. Easily stated, Max doesn't have the attention span to even notice if something has changed in the first place.

Tail End: The bottom line here, sometimes change is inevitable conquer with grace and determination and you will be just fine.

CHAPTER 9
THE ART OF LOVE

Somebody, a long, long, long time ago said that absence makes the heart grow fonder. Nobody really knows who quoted this phrase, but it was first published in Francis Davidson's *Poetical Rhapsody* in 1602, where the words appear as the first phase of a poem in the edition.

Unfortunately, the author of this poem was anonymous. It is amazing to me that in this day and age that this phrase continues to have a profound place in effect on our society.

I really believe absence does make the heart grow fonder and is a true measure of unconditional love. I found this out when I went on a vacation to the North Rim of the Grand Canyon. This trip entailed a 15-hour car drive and the same car stuffed so fully that there was barely enough room for my daughter which meant no room for the Pugs on this trip.

This forced me to search for a suitable doggie hotel for the Grumble. Great efforts were made in the research of such a facility. I needed to find a doggie hotel that would cater to every whim of my Pug babies and show them the love I give them every day. Or, at least, something very close to the same love. I needed to find a place that would provide regular exercise, feed them a proper diet and administer medication to Loretta and Rocco. Most importantly, we needed friendly faces that wouldn't put Gus into shock thinking that he was being taken back to a shelter.

After weeks of investigation found all of this and more at a pet ranch near my home. The staff was everything my fur babies possibly needed. In my eyes, it was a spa for my Pugs. They could have a pedicure, a bath, floofing, playtime, and much more. Their rooms were even nicer than some of the hotels we stayed at on our trip. I'm being totally serious.

Now, if you were to look at this week through the eyes of my Pug Babies I'm sure it was the polar opposite of my opinion. To them, it was a week of incarceration. I can just see them marking the days with their claws on the wall of their room as each day passed.

Ssscccccrrrrraaaaattttcccccccchhhhh. But I am sure each of them adjusted in their own way.

Let's start with Rocco. He is the most un-aggressive of the Grumble. In fact, when we go to the dog park to play, he pretty much spends most of his time sitting under the bench where I sit and watch the other dogs romp around and play with each other. The look on his face when he was sprung pretty much confirmed my suspicion that Loretta probably sold him for a pack of cigarettes. He came out with two tattoos on his front shoulders. The right side said "MOM" and the left side said "REBEL" It took weeks and weeks of therapy to get him through the trauma.

Loretta, on the other hand, within a day was running the entire joint. She was the boss, and nobody questioned it. When she walked out to the play area all the other dogs moved to the side giving her plenty of clearance to walk wherever she wanted. She probably hung around the bench press weight area and had small talk with her gang. She even had control over the warden. When Big Loretta spoke...everyone listened.

Now Gus was pretty much a fly on the wall. He didn't get sold for cigarettes and wasn't a leader. He was, however, working with the guards. He became an "Inside Pug informant". If only Loretta knew her bunkmate had more power than any other pup in the joint. He would disappear for a couple of hours here and there.

Little did anyone know that he was getting massages and eating gourmet meals. If he brought some juicy news to the guards, they would reward him with some extra-long games of fetch-the-hedgehog. He actually enjoyed his incarceration.

I am glad that they made it through this ordeal with the need of a minimal amount of "Pug therapy" and it seems the doggie hotel survived their stay as well. At least I think I can bring them back someday.

The look in the eyes of those Pugs upon release was nothing short of unconditional love. Love was bubbling and exploding out of their bodies. As I sat on the slippery linoleum floor the three slid and projected into the air and landed all over my body. One on my head, one on my belly, and the last slid into my side. I fell back with glee and could literally feel their love in the form of Pug kisses and Pug schmutz.

All is almost back to normal at home. Well, at least everything except the fact that Loretta still insists that we call her "Big Loretta"!

Tail End: In truth, absence did make the love grow stronger and I found that I was as happy to see them as they were to see me. I also observed that they are just as excited to see me after I have gone out for 3 min to check the mail. Does your pup miss you when you are away?

CHAPTER 10
THE ART OF WAGGING

As you may have noticed there was one Pug that was noticeably missing from all the other chapters. Believe it or not, that was intentional. As if you couldn't tell from the introductions to the Grumble, Daisy has forever left a place in my heart that will never be filled.

With that being said, I probably learned the most from Daisy. Lessons and observations from every chapter she taught me in less than the 2 years that she was with me.

Relaxing was a given. Her choice spot was under my chin on my chest. Of course, it hindered any kind of progress or work from home, but it did teach me to take some time and enjoy the Pugs and people I love.

Appreciation was obvious in Daisy. She thanked me every day for rescuing her. Her kind spirit emerged from her with every Daisy smile. I know she was thankful for her new home, nutritious food, and lots and lots of love. I could just feel it.

There was no doubt that Daisy exuded confidence. Her distinct saunter through the home, the vigor she expelled when she ate her meals. The strength she showed when I threw the ball and looked at me like I was crazy as if I thought she was going to chase that piece of tether. She had no problem ignoring my request. As matter of fact, she was very confident in her blatant disobedience to my command.

When you are a Pug owner you learn the subtleties of communication. Things are not black and white. To some, a staring look means one thing. To a Pug owner, you need to understand the Pug Communication Model. One single stare from Daisy could mean I'm too tired to close my eye while falling asleep, another interpretation is to feed me before I breathe my last breath and die right here in front of you, or, go get my tiara!

I'm sure you get it by now. It took years to learn to properly communicate with her and I use it every day to communicate with the current Grumble. It took patience, and some telepathy to hone this skill to the level that I understood everything Daisy was requesting.

Telling the truth was simple for Daisy. I'm pretty sure she did not know how to lie in the first place. I mean how could she? She never did anything to get into trouble to need to lie about. To put it simply, she kept her smushy nose clean.

Embracing change was pretty easy for Daisy, too. I'm not sure where she came from originally, but the day the foster parent brought her to my home I got down on the floor. The first thing she did was to run into the dining room, pee on the leg of the dining room table, run over to me, and then licked my face. She embraces change. She taught me to not fight change, but to embrace it!

Love is truly one of life's most amazing feelings. Daisy was 24 pounds of furry, snorty walking love. She made everyone who came into contact with her feel happy and good inside. When I would take her for walks, people in cars would slow down just to catch a glimpse of her.

It was even funnier when I would give her a ride in my old jogging stroller. After about a mile she would stop walking and just lay down. It didn't matter where she was, she would just stop. BS, (before stroller) this happened, and I had to carry all 24 pounds of her a quarter of a mile home. Let's just say that never happened again. Even as I struggled to carry that 24-pound package of love I couldn't be mad at her because she would look up at me like I had just saved her life.

I guess that is what love is all about. Doing something for someone or protecting them, caring for them and trusting each other. Daisy knew I had her back and I knew she had mine.

With all of this information on how to live your life to its fullest, I guess the easiest way to put it is to Wag More! If you take look at Pugs, mine at least, they are always wagging their tails. I talk to them -they wag, I feed them - they wag, I play with them-they wag. I have even noticed that sometimes they wag in their sleep. They manage to eliminate confrontation and have you ever noticed that when they do bark, it is usually at something simple? For example birds, leaves, dust, or the opening of a potato chip bag. They simply choose to wag. And so should we!

Tail End: As I continue to follow the lead of my grumble, I choose to live my life by the simple lessons and daily observations they have taught me. This is achieved by simply wagging more! Do you choose to Wag More!

ABOUT THE AUTHOR

The Woman of Wow, Kellen Ann, is em-"barking" on a new adventure! As the queen of Cards that, Kellen always knew the true royalty was the grumble at her feet.

Kellen Ann is an author and 3-Pug mom who has written her book, Wag More!, three times, now believing this third version in your hands to be the winner.

In Wag More!, she shares life lessons learned from a 'grumble' - a term defined in the book - which is essentially how she chose to work with her own demons. She believes that the silly, smushy-faced, snorkely creatures she's been surrounded by for years have taught her more than any expensive therapy ever could.

Being able to avoid making light of some tough feelings and reactions to abuse allowed Kellen to finally create the tongue-in-cheek book she envisioned.

Kellen Ann is an author, mother to Emily, the Queen of her Grumble. Born in Chicago and spending most of her adult life in California, Kellen has always been an entrepreneur at heart. After graduating from CSU Sacramento with a degree in Art, she chose to pursue a career as a commercial real estate broker - but as fate would have it, she would take advantage of the pandemic to combine her love of art and gratitude to start her own business, Cards that Wow! With the help from her supportive friends and mentors, Kellen was able to fulfill one of her lifelong goals by writing her first book. Her story is proof that no matter how hard your experiences may be or what you are told about yourself; if you believe in yourself anything is possible!

PUG LIFE

JOURNAL ENTRY

Join our community:
The Real Pugs That Wow!

Made in the USA
Columbia, SC
16 April 2023

b3d23438-d2db-4442-903c-b03dfd18702cR01